P9-DMA-888

This is Daniel Cook
on a Hike

Kids Can Press

This is Daniel Cook.
He likes to go different places,
meet interesting people and
try new things.

Mostly I like to have fun!

Today Daniel is going on a hike.

Here we are!

This is Amy. Amy is a naturalist. She's going to be Daniel's guide.

You can go on all sorts of hikes — short hikes and long hikes, day hikes and night hikes — in all sorts of places.

Let's go!

Before Daniel and Amy set out, they have to get ready.

Here's our checklist!

- Hiking boots or running shoes
- Hats
- Sunscreen — for ears, too, don't forget!
- Water
- Binoculars
- Bug spray — I hate mosquitoes!
- Compass

Binoculars are great for hiking. They make faraway objects appear closer, so you can observe, or watch, animals without disturbing them.

There!
Can you see
what I see?

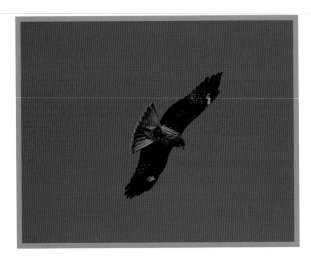

They're especially handy for bird watching. You can spy birds flying high in the sky!

Of course, you don't need binoculars all the time — there's plenty to see on a hike with your own two eyes!

Amy and Daniel are watching a damselfly.

This little blur is the damselfly!

Damselflies are related to dragonflies, but there are a few differences between them. A damselfly is smaller, and when it's at rest, its wings fold over its back. A dragonfly's wings stay straight out even when it's resting.

Both can be found near water.

You can observe many insects, such as damselflies, out in the open, but others are harder to find.

Look high and low — lots of insects like dark hiding spots. Turn over a rock and you might find beetles, a worm or ants. Ants like to make their nests underground. They dig tunnels and small rooms to lay their eggs in.

It's a tiny construction zone!

Look closely at plants and flowers, too. Bees are attracted to flowers' bright colors — they know they'll find nectar to drink.

Spittlebugs lay their eggs on plants' stalks and leaves.

And ladybugs eat aphids, smaller, plant-eating bugs.

That's 25 times taller than me!

Plants have been around for millions of years. Some plants have even survived since dinosaurs roamed the Earth! Today these horsetails are medium-sized plants, but 300 million years ago, they grew as tall as trees — about 30 m (100 ft.) tall. They were probably food for plant-eating dinosaurs!

Be sure to steer clear of some plants, though. Poison ivy might be pretty to look at, but you don't want to touch its leaves or berries. They cause red, itchy skin rashes. Remember: Leaves three, let it be. Berries white, take flight.

Scratching itches is no fun!

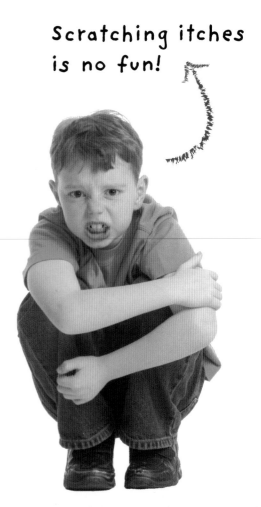

And *never* eat any wild berries, plants or fungi, such as mushrooms, unless an adult knows it's safe. Many *look* tasty, but they can make you very sick.

The poison in poison ivy and some fungi is a defense that helps plants survive.

When surprised, birds and animals will also defend themselves. Amy and Daniel watch quietly from a safe distance.

Most animals make noise to warn you to stay away. Some just stay still to blend into their surroundings. Skunks and porcupines have special ways of dealing with danger.

Pee-EW!

OUCH!

Birds will swoop down to scare off unwelcome visitors that are too close to their nest. They beat their wings and chatter and call loudly.

Listen for insects, animals and birds nearby!

Daniel and Amy noticed that there wasn't any noise coming from this robin's nest.

The nest is abandoned, so it's safe for us to take a closer look.

Trees are home to many animals, birds and insects.

They really are treehouses!

Conifers and deciduous trees are two kinds of tree families. Conifers grow new needles as the old ones fall off, so they look full year round.

Spring   Summer   Fall   Winter

Deciduous trees stand bare in the winter. But before their leaves fall, their colors turn from green to yellow, orange or red. In the spring, they grow new leaves.

Conifer seeds look different from deciduous seeds. Conifers drop cones that you'll find on a fall or winter hike.

Deciduous seeds come in many different packages. In the spring, look for keys helicoptering from maple trees.

In the fall, watch for acorns dropping out of oak trees.

And bite into an apple to find apple tree seeds, called pips, inside!

When those trees grow up, they'll make shady resting spots after a hike!

The next time I go hiking I'm going to make some tasty granola track snacks to bring along — you can, too!

You will need
- 500 mL   rolled oats   2 cups
- 25 mL   sunflower seeds   1/8 cup
- 375 mL   mixed, dried fruit   1 1/2 cups
- 1 mL   cinnamon   1/4 tsp.
- 125 mL   honey   1/4 cup
- 50 mL   butter, melted   4 tbsp.

1. Ask a grown-up to set the oven to 300°F.

I like dried apples, apricots and cranberries.

2. In a bowl, mix the oats, sunflower seeds, cinnamon and dried fruit.

3. Ask a grown-up to melt the butter. Stir the butter and honey together and pour it onto the oat mixture. Mix well.

4. With a grown-up's help, spread the mixture onto a cookie sheet and bake for 15 – 20 minutes, or until golden.

5. Let cool. Then break up the mixture into small pieces — time for the taste test!

Yummy!

Based on the TV series *This is Daniel Cook*. Concept created by J.J. Johnson and Blair Powers. Produced by marblemedia and Sinking Ship Productions Inc.

Text © 2006 Marble Media Inc.
Illustrations © 2006 Kids Can Press Ltd.

THIS IS DANIEL COOK, EPS #123 © 2004 Short Order Cook TV I Inc.

All rights reserved. No part of this publication may be reproduced, stored in a retrieval system or transmitted, in any form or by any means, without the prior written permission of Kids Can Press Ltd. or, in case of photocopying or other reprographic copying, a license from The Canadian Copyright Licensing Agency (Access Copyright). For an Access Copyright license, visit www.accesscopyright.ca or call toll free to 1-800-893-5777.

Neither the Publisher nor the Author shall be liable for any damage that may be caused or sustained as a result of conducting any of the activities in this book without specifically following instructions, conducting the activities without proper supervision, or ignoring the cautions contained in the book.

Kids Can Press acknowledges the financial support of the Government of Ontario, through the Ontario Media Development Corporation's Ontario Book Initiative; the Ontario Arts Council; the Canada Council for the Arts; and the Government of Canada, through the BPIDP, for our publishing activity.

The producers of *This is Daniel Cook* acknowledge the support of Treehouse TV, TVOntario, other broadcast and funding partners and the talented, hard-working crew that made *This is Daniel Cook* a reality. In addition, they acknowledge the support and efforts of Deb, Murray and the Cook family, as well as Karen Boersma, Sheila Barry and Valerie Hussey at Kids Can Press.

Published in Canada by
Kids Can Press Ltd.
29 Birch Avenue
Toronto, ON M4V 1E2

Published in the U.S. by
Kids Can Press Ltd.
2250 Military Road
Tonawanda, NY 14150

www.kidscanpress.com

Written by Yvette Ghione
Edited by Karen Li
Illustrations and design by Céleste Gagnon
With special thanks to Amy Wilson of the Island Natural Science School

Printed and bound in China

The hardcover edition of this book is smyth sewn casebound.
The paperback edition of this book is limp sewn with a drawn-on cover.

Kids Can Press is a *Corus*™ Entertainment company

CM 06 0 9 8 7 6 5 4 3 2 1
CM PA 06 0 9 8 7 6 5 4 3 2 1

Visit Daniel online at **www.thisisdanielcook.com**

Library and Archives Canada Cataloguing in Publication

Ghione, Yvette

    This is Daniel Cook on a hike / written by Yvette Ghione.

ISBN-13: 978-1-55453-079-3 (bound)
ISBN-10: 1-55453-079-2 (bound)
ISBN-13: 978-1-55453-080-9 (pbk.)
ISBN-10: 1-55453-080-6 (pbk.)

1. Hiking—Juvenile literature.   2. Nature—Juvenile literature.
I. Title.

QH48.G49 2006   j796.51   C2006-900739-X

Photo Credits

Every reasonable effort has been made to trace ownership of, and give accurate credit to, copyrighted material. Information that would enable the publisher to correct any discrepancies in future editions would be appreciated.

p. 5: (trail head) © iStockphoto.com/justmeproductions;
p. 11: (ants) Walter Meayers Edwards/National Geographic/Getty Images; p. 12: (spittlebug) Bill Beatty/Visuals Unlimited;
p. 14: (poison ivy) © iStockphoto.com/oddrose;
p. 20: (acorns, pine cones) © PhotoDisc, (green maple tree key) © iStockphoto.com/jsp, (brown maple tree key) © iStockphoto.com/anettelinnea, (apple) © PhotoDisc;
THIS IS DANIEL COOK gallery photos by Cylla Von Tiedemann;
THIS IS DANIEL COOK location photos by Peter Stranks; all remaining photos © 2006 Jupiterimages Corporation.